Swansea C
Quiz Boo

101 Questions To Test Your Knowledge
Of Swansea City Football Club

Published by Glowworm Press
7 Nuffield Way
Abingdon OX14 1RL

By Chris Carpenter

Swansea City Football Club

This Swansea City Football Club quiz book contains one hundred and one informative and entertaining trivia questions with multiple choice answers. Some of the questions are easy, yet most are quite challenging, and this entertaining book is guaranteed to test your knowledge and memory of the club's long history.

You will be asked a large variety of wonderful questions on a wide range of topics associated with Swansea City FC for you to test yourself. You will be quizzed on players, legends, managers, opponents, transfer deals, trophies, records, honours, fixtures and much more, guaranteeing you an educational experience and hours of fun. Informative, enjoyable and fun, this quiz book will test your knowledge of **Swansea City Football Club** and prove you know the club well.

2020/21 Season Edition

FOREWORD

When I was asked to write a foreword to this book I was flattered.

I have known Chris the author for many years and his knowledge of facts and figures and football in general is phenomenal.

His love for the game and his talent for writing quiz books makes him the ideal man to pay homage to my real true love Swansea City Football Club.

This book came about as a result of a challenge in a pub!

I do hope you enjoy the book.

Gareth Phillips

Let's start with some relatively easy questions.

1. When was Swansea founded; as Swansea Town?
    A. 1892
    B. 1902
    C. 1912

2. When did the club change its name from Swansea Town to Swansea City?
    A. 1949
    B. 1959
    C. 1969

3. What is Swansea City's nickname?
    A. The Ducks
    B. The Geese
    C. The Swans

4. Where does Swansea City play their home games?
    A. Freedom Arena
    B. Liberty Stadium
    C. Pleasure Dome

5. What is the stadium's capacity?
    A. 20,520
    B. 20,827
    C. 21,088

6. Who or what is the club mascot?
    A. Cyril the Swan
    B. Meryl the Swan
    C. Sheryl the Swan

7. Who has made the most appearances for the club in total?
    A. Ivor Allchurch
    B. Wilfred Milne
    C. Herbie Williams

8. Who has made the most post-war appearances for the club?
    A. Leon Britton
    B. Roger Freestone
    C. Robbie James

9. Who is the club's record goal scorer?
    A. Ivor Allchurch
    B. Gwynn Davies
    C. Rodney Marsh

10. Which of these is a "traditional" pub near the ground?
    A. The Locomotive
    B. The Railway Inn
    C. The Station

OK, so here are the answers to the first ten questions. If you get eight or more right, you are doing well but, be warned, the questions will get harder.

A1. The club was founded in 1912, as Swansea Town.

A2. The club changed its name to Swansea City in 1969, when Swansea was granted city status.

A3. Swansea City's nickname is officially the Swans, although they are also known as the Jacks.

A4. Swansea City play their home games at the Liberty Stadium.

A5. The current stadium capacity is 21,088; although there are plans to increase this.

A6. The club mascot is of course Cyril the Swan. Give yourself a bonus point if you knew his "wife" was called Cybil.

A7. Wilfred Milne holds the record for most ever appearances for the club, making a grand total of 586 appearances between 1920 and 1937.

A8. Goalkeeper Roger Freestone has made the most appearances for the club since the war. He played in 566 first-team matches before retiring in 2004. He only cost £45,000 when he was bought from Chelsea, so that was money well spent I am sure you will agree.

A9. Ivor Allchurch is Swansea City's record goal scorer of all time with 166 goals in all competitions. Legend.

A10. It would be fair to say the area around the ground is not blessed with good pubs. It is best to either drink in the stadium itself, the city centre or track down the Railway Inn, which is ten minutes' walk from the ground. Be prepared to queue for a pint though.

OK, back to the questions.

11. What is the record transfer fee paid?
    A. £14 million
    B. £16 million
    C. £18 million

12. Who was the record transfer fee paid for?
    A. Andre Ayew
    B. Borja Baston
    C. Wilfried Bony

13. What is the record transfer fee received?
    A. £41 million
    B. £43 million
    C. £45 million

14. Who was the record transfer fee received for?
    A. Wilfred Bony
    B. Gylfi Sigurdsson
    C. Scott Sinclair

15. Who was the first Swansea City player to play for Wales?
    A. Billy Hole
    B. Ivor Jones
    C. Dai Nicholas

16. Who has won the most international caps whilst a Swansea City player?
    A. Dennis Lawrence
    B. Ki Sung-yueng
    C. Ashley Williams

17. Who has scored the most international goals?
    A. Ivor Allchurch
    B. Walter Boyd
    C. Trevor Ford

18. Who has scored the most hat tricks for Swansea?
    A. Ivor Allchurch
    B. Jack Fowler
    C. Bob Latchford

19. Who is the youngest player ever to represent the club?
    A. Nigel Dalling
    B. Nat Palling
    C. Nick Smalling

20. Who is the oldest player ever to represent the club?
    A. Roger Freestone
    B. Tommy Hutchison
    C. Al McKinnon

Here are the answers to the last set of questions.

A11. Swansea City paid £18 million for a Ghanian striker, which is their record transfer.

A12. The fee of £18 million was paid to West Ham United for Andre Ayew in January 2018. It eclipsed the previous transfer record of £15.5 million paid to Atletico Madrid for Borja Baston in August 2016.

A13. The record transfer fee received by Swansea City is £45 million.

A14. The record transfer fee of £45 million was received from Everton City in August 2017 for Gylfi Sigurdsson.

A15. Ivor Jones was the first Swansea City player to play for Wales. He made his debut back in 1920 and went on to play ten times for his country.

A16. Ashley Williams won 64 caps for Wales whilst at Swansea City, and is thus the most capped international player in the club's history.

A17. Both Ivor Allchurch and Trevor Ford scored 23 international goals for Wales.

A18. Jack Fowler scored 9 hat tricks in his time at the club, between 1924 and 1927.

A19. Nigel Dalling is the youngest player ever to represent the club. He made his first team debut at the age of 15 years and 289 days against Southport on 6th December 1974.

A20. Tommy Hutchison is the oldest player ever to represent the club. He appeared for the club at the age of 43 years and 172 days against Southend United on 12th March 1991.

Now we move onto some questions about some of the club's records.

21. What is the club's record win in any competition?
      A. 10-0
      B. 11-0
      C. 12-0

22. Who did they beat?
      A. Shamrock Rovers
      B. Sligo Rovers
      C. Sliema Wanderers

23. In which season?
      A. 1962/63
      B. 1972/73
      C. 1982/83

24. What is the club's record win in the league?
      A. 7-0
      B. 8-0
      C. 9-0

25. Who did they beat?
      A. Halifax
      B. Hartlepool
      C. Hull

26. In which season?
      A. 1957/58
      B. 1967/68
      C. 1977/78

27. What is the club's record defeat?
    A. 0-7
    B. 0-8
    C. 0-9

28. Which of these players made into the PFA team of the year three times?
    A. Chris Coleman
    B. Jason Scotland
    C. Lee Trundle

29. What is the club's record attendance ever?
    A. 30,796
    B. 32,796
    C. 34,796

30. What is the club's record attendance in the new ground?
    A. 20,718
    B. 20,854
    C. 20,992

Here are the answers to the last set of questions.

A21. The club's record win in any competition is 12-0.

A22. The club thrashed Sliema Wanderers from Malta in the European Cup Winners Cup.

A23. The record 12-1 victory took place on 15th September 1982, so therefore it was in the 1982/83 season.

A24. The club's record win in the League is 8-0.

A25. The record win was against Hartlepool in the old Fourth Division.

A26. The record 8-0 victory took place on 1st April 1978, so it was in the 1977/78 season.

A27. The club's record defeat in any competition is 0-8. Liverpool beat Swansea by that score in an FA Cup game in January 1990 as did Monaco in a European Cup Winners Cup match in October 1991.

A28. Lee Trundle was voted into the PFA team of the year three times. 2004, 2005 and 2006 are the years Trundle was in his prime and recognised by his peers.

A29. Swansea City's record home attendance ever was 32,796 at the Vetch Field in an FA Cup 4th round match against Arsenal on 17th February 1968.

A30. Swansea City's record home attendance at the new stadium is 20,992 against Liverpool in the Premier League on 1st May 2016.

Let's give you some easier questions.

31. What is the traditional colour of the home shirt?
    A. Blue
    B. Red
    C. White

32. What is the traditional colour of the away shirt?
    A. Orange
    B. Purple
    C. Red

33. Who is the current club sponsor?
    A. Bet UK
    B. Swansea University
    C. Yobet

34. Who was the first club shirt sponsor?
    A. Action
    B. Diversified Products
    C. Gulf Oil

35. Which of these sports brands is the current kit supplier to the club?
    A. Adidas
    B. Joma
    C. Umbro

36. Which of these sports brands has not supplied kit to Swansea City?
    A. Adidas
    B. Nike

C. Le Coq Sportif

37. Who was the club's first foreign signing?
    A. Dico Schteuber
    B. Nico Schroder
    C. Rico Schumacher

38. Who was the club's first black player?
    A. Cliff Hardenborough
    B. Steve Mardenborough
    C. Winston Pardonborough

39. Who started the 2020/21 season as manager?
    A. Steve Cooper
    B. Paul Clement
    C. Graham Potter

40. Who is the club captain for the 2020/21 season?
    A. Ben Cabango
    B. Matt Grimes
    C. Wayne Routledge

Here are the answers to the last set of questions.

A31. The traditional colour of the home shirt is of course white.

A32. The traditional colour of the away shirt is a difficult one, but it is fair to say that red has been the predominant colour worn more than any other colour.

A33. Swansea University is the current shirt sponsor of Swansea City, having signed a deal in August 2020.

A34. Diversified Products (DP) were the first shirt sponsor of Swansea City, back in the 1986/87 season.

A35. Joma is the current kit supplier to the club.

A36. Nike has never supplied kit to Swansea City whereas Adidas and Le Coq Sportif, amongst others, have.

A37. Goalkeeper Nico Schroder was the club's first foreign signing. He made his solitary league appearance at Stockport in August 1976.

A38. Midfielder Steve Mardenborough was the club's first black player. In the 1984/85 season he made 36 league appearances and scored 7 goals.

A39. Steve Cooper started the 2020/21 season as manager. He was appointed in June 2019.

A40. Midfielder Matt Grimes started the 2020/21 season as captain.

Right, onto the next set of questions.

41. Who is the club's longest serving manager of all time?
    A. Joe Bradshaw
    B. Trevor Morris
    C. John Toshack

42. Who was the club's first foreign manager?
    A. Roberto Martinez
    B. Jan Molby
    C. Paulo Sousa

43. What is the name of the match day programme?
    A. Swansea City official matchday programme
    B. Swansea City Diaries
    C. The Swan

44. What is the official Swansea City website?
    A. swans.co.uk
    B. swanseafc.com
    C. swanseacity.net

45. Which of these is a Swansea City fanzine?
    A. Not the view
    B. Swansea Oh Swansea
    C. When Skies are Grey

46. What type of animal is on the club crest?
    A. Reptile
    B. Mammal

C. Bird

47. What is the club's motto?
    A. Consectatio Excellentiae
    B. Nil Satis Nisi Optimum
    C. No motto

48. Who is considered as Swansea City's main rivals?
    A. Bristol City
    B. Cardiff City
    C. Newport County

49. Who scored the most goals in a season in all competitions?
    A. Robbie James
    B. Cyril Pearce
    C. Herbie Williams

50. Who is currently the club chairman?
    A. Trevor Birch
    B. Huw Jenkins
    C. Julian Winter

Here are the answers to the last set of questions.

A41. Trevor Morris is the club's longest serving manager of all time. He served from August 1958 to May 1965 and he managed 327 matches.

A42. Dane Jan Molby was the club's first foreign manager, taking office on the 22nd February 1996. He was in charge for 80 games in total.

A43. The catchy name of the match day programme is 'Swansea City official matchday programme'.

A44. swanseacity.net is the address of the club's official website and it is very a comprehensive website which is updated daily.

A45. Swansea Oh Swansea is considered the best known of the Swansea City fanzines.

A46. Swansea City's badge consists of a stylised bird.

A47. Unusually for a football club, Swansea City does not have an official motto.

A48. Cardiff City is of course considered as Swansea City's main rival.

A49. Cyril Pearce holds the record for most goals scored in a season. He banged in 40 goals in the 1930/31 season, including 35 in the league.

A50. Julian Winter is the current chairman and chief executive. He took up the position in September 2020.

Here is the next set of questions.

51. When did the club win the League Cup?
    A. 2012
    B. 2013
    C. 2014

52. Who did they beat in the final?
    A. Birmingham City
    B. Bradford City
    C. Bristol City

53. What was the score?
    A. 3-0
    B. 4-0
    C. 5-0

54. Who was the manager when the club won the League Cup?
    A. Michael Laudrup
    B. Roberto Martinez
    C. Brendan Rodgers

55. In the run to the League Cup final how many games did they play, excluding the final itself?
    A. 5
    B. 6
    C. 7

56. How many seasons has the club been in the Premier League in total?
    A. 6
    B. 7

C. 8

57. Who is Swansea City's highest ever goal scorer in a Premier League season?
     A. Wilfried Bony
     B. Michu
     C. Wayne Routledge

58. What is the club's best ever finish in the Premier League?
     A. 7th
     B. 8th
     C. 9th

59. Who was the manager as Swansea recorded their best ever Premier League finish?
     A. Garry Monk
     B. Michael Laudrup
     C. Brendan Rodgers

60. What is the record number of points the club has achieved in a Premier League season?
     A. 52
     B. 54
     C. 56

Here are your answers to the last ten questions.

A51. Swansea City won the League Cup on the 24th February 2013.

A52. Swansea defeated Bradford City in the final at Wembley Stadium.

A53. Swansea won the final 5-0, with goals coming from Michu (one) and with Dyer and De Guzman both scoring twice. The Swans were 2-0 up at half time, led 4-0 after an hour, with the final goal coming in injury time.

A54. Dane Michael Laudrup was the manager that day, and the whole season for that matter.

A55. To reach the final, Swansea played six games, including the two legged semi-final against Chelsea. None of the games went to extra time, or penalties.

A56. Swansea's first campaign in the Premier League was the 2011/12 season, and the club was ever present until 2017/18, so that's seven in total.

A57. Michu scored 18 league goals in the 2012/2013 Premier League season.

A58. The club's best finish ever in the Premier League was the 2014/15 season when they finished 8th.

A59. Garry Monk led the Swans to their best ever finish in the Premier League in the 2014/15 season.

A60. In finishing 8th, the club amassed their highest number of points in the top flight with 56.

Here is the next set of questions, let's hope you get most of them right.

61. What is the highest number of goals that Swansea City has scored in a league season?
    A. 90
    B. 91
    C. 92

62. What is the fewest number of goals that Swansea City has conceded in a league season?
    A. 33
    B. 36
    C. 39

63. How many times have Swansea won the Welsh Cup?
    A. 8
    B. 9
    C. 10

64. When did Swansea first win the Welsh Cup?
    A. 1913
    B. 1933
    C. 1953

65. How many times have the club won the Welsh Youth Cup?
    A. 6
    B. 8
    C. 10

66. What is the record number of points the club has achieved in a season, ever?
    A. 90
    B. 92
    C. 94

67. What is the club's best ever finish in the old First Division?
    A. 6th
    B. 7th
    C. 8th

68. How many times have Swansea City played European football?
    A. 1
    B. 5
    C. 8

69. In the 2013/14 Europa League campaign, which of these sides did Swansea play?
    A. Napoli
    B. St Gallen
    C. Valencia

70. Who did the club beat to reach the 2013/14 Europa League group stage?
    A. Braga
    B. Magdeburg
    C. Petrolul Ploiesti

Here are the answers to the last set of questions.

A61. Swansea City scored 92 goals in 46 matches in the old Fourth Division in the 1976/77 season.

A62. Swansea City conceded just 36 goals in 42 matches in the old Second Division in the 1983/84 season.

A63. Swansea has won the Welsh Cup a total of ten times.

A64. Swansea first Welsh Cup victory, which they won as Swansea Town, was in 1913.

A65. The club have won the FAW Welsh Youth Cup a total of ten times, most recently in 2016.

A66. Swansea amassed 92 points during the 2007/08 season in League One.

A67. Swansea finished an incredible 6th in the old First Division in the 1981/82 season, having been promoted the season before.

A68. Swansea City has played in eight European campaigns. They qualified seven times by virtue of winning the Welsh Cup, and once for winning the League Cup.

A69. Swansea City played all three of these clubs in the 2013/14 Europa League. Give yourself a bonus point if you knew that.

A70. Swansea defeated Romanian side Petrolul Ploiesti 6-3 on aggregate to reach the Europa League group stage.

Now let's have some ground related questions.

71. Why was Vetch Field so called?
      A. After Lord Vetch who owned the land
      B. A plant called vetch used to grow there
      C. It was in a valley of the River Vetch

72. Who scored the last ever league goal at Vetch Field?
      A. Adrian Forbes
      B. Leighton James
      C. Andy Robinson

73. How many internationals were played in total at Vetch Field?
      A. 12
      B. 15
      C. 18

74. What is the current state of the Vetch?
      A. Allotments
      B. Housing
      C. Shopping centre

75. Who performed at the Vetch in 1976?
      A. The Rolling Stones
      B. Stevie Wonder
      C. The Who

76. Who performed at the Liberty Stadium in 2014?
      A. JLS
      B. Kings of Leon
      C. Rod Stewart

77. Where is the away end of the Liberty Stadium?
    A. East Stand
    B. North Stand
    C. South Stand

78. Which rugby club does Swansea City share the ground with?
    A. Eagles
    B. Hawks
    C. Ospreys

79. Which stand is the largest?
    A. The East Stand
    B. The South Stand
    C. The West Stand

80. Why is the ground called the Liberty Stadium?
    A. After Lord Liberty
    B. After Liberty Properties
    C. Chosen by most votes in an online competition

Here are the ground related answers.

A71. Before Swansea Town was established, local children would play football on waste ground where the ground was eventually built, in which a plant, called "vetch" (a type of legume) was grown.

A72. Adrian Forbes scored the last ever league goal at the Vetch in Swansea's 1-0 win over Shrewsbury Town on 30th April 2005.

A73. 18 internationals were played at Vetch Field, including two World Cup qualifiers. The last international to be played there was on 19th October 1988 as Wales drew 2-2 with Finland in a World Cup qualifying match.

A74. Over 10 years since the last game was played at the Vetch, the local council have still not decided what to do with the space. A "community orchard" , open space and a small housing development are currently being considered as part of the so called "masterplan". At present part of the old ground is an allotment where locals grow fruit and vegetables.

A75. On the 12th June 1976, The Who played at the Vetch. Tickets cost just £4.   Stevie Wonder played the stadium in 1984.

A76. On the 2nd July 2014, Kings of Leon played at the Liberty Stadium. Rod Stewart and JLS played on separate nights at the stadium in 2011.

A77. Away fans are housed in the North Stand.

A78. Ospreys Rugby Club ground-share with Swansea City.

A79. The West Stand is the largest in the ground. It contains the dug-outs, tunnels to the dressing rooms, the technical areas and executive boxes at the top of the seats in the upper tier. The West Stand also contains the TV studio, on the 3rd floor.

A80. On the 18th October 2005, local developers Liberty Properties plc won the naming rights to call it "Liberty Stadium". In UEFA matches, it is called Swansea Stadium due to UEFA regulations on sponsorship.

I hope you're learning some new facts about the club. Here is the next batch of ten questions.

81. What is the size of the pitch?
    A. 105x70 yards
    B. 110x72 yards
    C. 115x74 yards

82. Where is Swansea City's training ground?
    A. Land Ahoy
    B. Landore
    C. Land Grab

83. Who started the 2020/21 season as goalkeeping coach?
    A. Martyn Margetson
    B. Michel Vorm
    C. Dorus de Vries

84. What is a famous song associated with the club?
    A. Hymns and Arias
    B. Just Can't Get Enough
    C. Keep The White Flag Flying High

85. What percentage of the club is owned by the Swansea City Supporters Trust?
    A. 20
    B. 25
    C. 30

86. What position did the club finish at the end of the 2019/2020 season?
    A. 4th

B. 5th
C. 6th

87. Which club did Jamal Lowe join from?
    A. Charlton Athletic
    B. Oldham Athletic
    C. Wigan Athletic

88. What is the club's official twitter account?
    A. @Swansea
    B. @SwanseaFC
    C. @SwansOfficial

89. Who is the highest goal scorer in the League for the club in a season in the top division?
    A. Ivor Allchurch
    B. Robbie James
    C. Bob Latchford

90. Who is Head of Recruitment?
    A. Steve Rands
    B. Andy Scott
    C. David Tivey

Here are the answers to the last ten questions.

A81. The size of the pitch is 115 yards long by 74 yards wide. By way of comparison, Wembley's pitch is 115 yards long by 75 yards wide.

A82. Based in the shadow of the Liberty Stadium, the Swans train at the multi million pound facility at Landore.

A83. Martyn Margetson started the 2020/21 season as goalkeeping coach, having been appointed to the role in June 2019.

A84. Hymns and Arias is a popular fans' chant. Altogether now, "And we were singing; Hymns and Arias; Land of my Fathers; Ar Hyd y Nos."

A85. The Trust currently owns 20% of Swansea City FC. Amongst other things, the trust has one permanent member of the football club board whose role is to represent the views of the fans.

A86. The club finished in 6th position at the end of the 2019/20 season.

A87. Winger Jamal Lowe joined Swansea from Wigan Athletic in August 2020 for a reported £800,000.

A88. @SwansOfficial is the club's official twitter account. It tweets multiple times a day, and it has over a million followers.

A89. Bob Latchford scored 34 League goals in the old First Division in the 1982/83 season.

A90. Andy Scott holds the role of Head of Recruitment at the club. He took up the job in July 2019.

Here is the final set of questions. Enjoy!

91. What animal is on the club crest?
    A. A duck
    B. A goose
    C. A swan

92. What was the title of the 2014 movie about the club?
    A. The Ace Of Spades
    B. The Black Swan
    C. Jack to a King

93. Who is Freddie Woodman on loan from?
    A. Middlesbrough
    B. Newcastle United
    C. Sunderland

94. What shirt number does Kyle Naughton wear?
    A. 2
    B. 6
    C. 26

95. Where was Kristoffer Peterson born?
    A. Denmark
    B. Norway
    C. Sweden

96. What shirt number has been permanently retired by the club?
    A. 20
    B. 30
    C. 40

97. Who was the first Swansea player to be capped by Wales?
    A. Rhys Davies
    B. Ivor Jones
    C. Owen Thomas

98. What shirt number did Garry Monk wear during his playing days at the club?
    A. 14
    B. 15
    C. 16

99. Who is the Club's honorary club president?
    A. Alan Curtis
    B. Ian Curtis
    C. John Curtis

100. Who can be considered the club's most successful manager?
    A. Frank Burrows
    B. Billy McCandless
    C. John Toshack

101. There is a statue of which legend outside the ground?
    A. Ivor Allchurch
    B. Chris Coleman
    C. Cliff Jones

Here goes with the final set of answers.

A91. Easy question. Of course it's a swan that is on the club crest. A black swan. At one time the swan was red, but it returned to being black in 2002.

A92. Jack to a King was a movie which focused on the club's rise from almost going out of business in 2001 to the glamour of the Premier League in 2011.

A93. Goalkeeper Woodman is currently on loan from Newcastle United.

A94. Naughton wears shirt number 26.

A95. Winger Peterson was born in Gothenburg, Sweden.

A96. Shirt number 40 has been permanently retired to honour Besian Idrizaj who died from a heart attack in aged just 22 in May 2010.

A97. Ivor Jones was the first Swansea player to be capped by Wales. He made his debut against Ireland on 14th February 1920.

A98. Garry Monk wore shirt number 16 for the club. He played a grand total of 226 games for the club, and he managed to play in all four divisions of professional football from 2004 to 2014, the majority of that time as captain. Legend.

A99. Alan Curtis was appointed to the role of honorary life president in May 2019.

A100. Under John Toshack, the club won 3 promotions, and three Welsh Cups, and he is considered by many to be the club's most successful manager. The club played some lovely football with Toshack in charge too.

A101. The magnificent bronze statue outside the ground is of course that of Ivor Allchurch.

That's a great question to finish with. I hope you enjoyed this book, and I hope you got most of the answers right.

I also hope you learnt one or two new things about the club.

If you saw anything wrong, please contact us via the glowwormpress.com website.

Thanks for reading, and for showing your support for this great club, would you be so kind as to leave a positive review on Amazon.

Printed in Great Britain
by Amazon